Original title:
After the Tears

Copyright © 2024 Swan Charm
All rights reserved.

Author: Sebastian Sarapuu
ISBN HARDBACK: 978-9916-89-874-1
ISBN PAPERBACK: 978-9916-89-875-8
ISBN EBOOK: 978-9916-89-876-5

Rays of Enlightenment

In the stillness, wisdom flows,
Guiding hearts where love bestows.
With every breath, a longing prayer,
In sacred silence, souls lay bare.

Awakening eyes to truths so bright,
Shattering darkness with holy light.
Each moment a gift, a chance to see,
The path of grace that sets us free.

The Harmony of Healing

In gentle whispers, peace resides,
A soothing balm for weary tides.
Hands lifted high, in faith we stand,
Together, bound by love's own hand.

With every heartbeat, healing flows,
Through trials faced, our spirit grows.
In unity, we find our way,
A brighter dawn with each new day.

The Sacred Veil Unfolds

As twilight mists begin to part,
Revealing wonders, filling heart.
In shadows cast, the light will play,
A sacred dance, a grand display.

The veil between the worlds so thin,
Invites us close to secrets within.
With open minds, we tread the line,
In every corner, love will shine.

The Light in the Gloom

When storms arise, and hope seems lost,
The heart must bear the bitter cost.
Yet in the depths, a glow persists,
A beacon bright, the spirit lifts.

Through valleys deep, where shadows creep,
A whispered promise, strong and steep.
In every trial, let courage bloom,
For in the night, we find our room.

Transcending the Storm

In the heart of fury, we stand so tall,
Faith our anchor, we won't let it fall.
Waves may crash and shadows may loom,
Yet in His promise, we find our bloom.

Whispers of hope amid the thunder's roar,
Guided by love, we shall fear no more.
Hands of grace reach through raging night,
Our souls uplifted, embracing the light.

The Spirit's Renewal

In the stillness, where silence sings,
A breath of peace, the spirit brings.
Worn and weary, we seek the grace,
To feel His presence, in this sacred space.

Like rivers flowing, His love cascades,
Healing our hearts, through darkened glades.
Each dawn is a promise, a brand new start,
Renewing our souls, igniting the heart.

Embraced by Divine Light

O gentle light, that softly shines,
Drawing our souls, in holy designs.
Wrap us in warmth, in love's sweet embrace,
Guiding our journeys through time and space.

In shadows cast, we seek Your glow,
Illuminating paths, where hope can grow.
With every heartbeat, let us ignite,
The flame of faith, embraced by Your light.

Echoes of Forgiveness

In the depths of sorrow, hard walls we build,
Yet mercy lingers, hearts can be filled.
Let go of the burden that weighs us down,
Wear the cloak of love, not the thorny crown.

Each word of kindness, a step towards peace,
In the embrace of grace, our troubles cease.
Echoes of forgiveness, sweet songs of grace,
Renewing our spirits in this sacred space.

The Cross of Forgotten Wounds

In shadows deep, we feel the pain,
Each tear a story, a silent strain.
Yet through the night, a light will gleam,
Hope rises softly, like a dream.

The cross we bear, a heavy load,
Yet love surrounds us, on this road.
A whisper calls, through endless strife,
In every wound, there blooms new life.

Forgiveness flows, like gentle streams,
Washing away our broken dreams.
With faith as our guide, we find our way,
In forgotten wounds, we learn to pray.

Each suffering soul, a treasure vast,
In trials faced, our spirits cast.
Through nails and thorns, the heart will mend,
With grace bestowed, on Him depend.

So let us rise, from earth to skies,
With lifted hearts, we magnify.
For in the cross, our burdens cease,
And in His love, we find our peace.

A Testament of Renewal

In every dawn, a promise grows,
A testament to life, it shows.
Awakening hearts, refreshed and new,
In every breath, the spirit too.

From ashes raised, we start again,
The past behind, released from pain.
The sun arises, bright and bold,
In light of grace, our stories told.

With open hands, we seek the light,
A journey shared, through day and night.
In every step, a sacred spark,
Guiding us through the fleeting dark.

Embrace the change, let spirits soar,
For every closing, opens doors.
A cycle spins, both near and far,
As life unfolds, our guiding star.

A song of hope within us sings,
Of love that blooms, and freedom brings.
In every heartbeat, renewal's song,
A testament true, where we belong.

Embraced by the Divine

In whispered prayers, we seek the grace,
To feel His warmth, to find our place.
With open arms, the heavens reach,
In stillness found, the soul will teach.

Through trials faced, and burdens shared,
We rise anew, for love has dared.
Each moment's breath, a sacred kiss,
Encased in faith, we find our bliss.

In shadows cast, His light breaks free,
A guiding hand, we long to see.
With every tear, a promise flows,
In love's embrace, the spirit grows.

With every heartbeat, a holy tune,
In darkness deep, we find the moon.
A light that shines, through pain and grace,
Embraced by love, our sacred space.

In the dance of life, we trust His plan,
For every step, we learn to stand.
When lost in doubt, His grace we find,
In the arms of the Divine, we're intertwined.

The Path of Unseen Blessings

Upon the path where shadows dwell,
Unseen blessings in silence swell.
In every challenge, a lesson glows,
The heart can nurture what faith sows.

With weary feet, we tread the ground,
In humble whispers, the truth is found.
Each stumble holds a sacred grace,
For hidden gifts, we must embrace.

As seasons change, we learn to see,
The beauty born in humility.
With hope as our guide, we journey on,
Through fading dusk, till break of dawn.

The road less traveled leads us home,
In quiet moments, we are not alone.
With every turn and every bend,
The path unfolds, our souls transcend.

Through blessings veiled, a truth stands tall,
In unity found, we rise and fall.
For in the unseen, we shall find,
The path of grace, forever kind.

The Calm After the Storm

In shadows deep where tempests raged,
A light emerged, the battle staged.
The winds subsided, silence fell,
A whispered peace, the heart's own swell.

The skies once dark, now painted blue,
With every breath, I start anew.
The rain has quenched the fiery thirst,
In calm I find my spirit's burst.

From chaos born, a strength divine,
In stillness, faith begins to shine.
Each droplet's fall a sacred rite,
From grief to joy, I find the light.

The Celestial Embrace

In twilight's glow, the stars align,
A gentle touch, your hand in mine.
Each whispered prayer, a soft caress,
In cosmic arms, we find our rest.

The moonlit path, we tread so light,
With every step, we chase the night.
A dance of souls, entwined so free,
In love's embrace, eternally.

The heavens sing, a sweet refrain,
With cosmic chords that ease our pain.
In silence shared, our spirits soar,
Together bound, forevermore.

Vows of Resilience

In trials faced, we vow to stand,
With hearts aflame, we hold His hand.
Through storms that swirl and darkness creep,
In faith we find our strength to keep.

With every tear, a lesson learned,
The fires of hope within us burned.
Together now, we rise anew,
With steadfast hearts, our dreams pursue.

In whispered faith, our spirits rise,
Through valleys low and endless skies.
With love as guide, we journey on,
In unity, our fears are gone.

Mourners' Symphony

In shadows cast, the mourners stand,
With heavy hearts and clasped hands.
A symphony of loss unfolds,
In grief we find what love beholds.

Each tear that falls, a note of pain,
A melody of joy and strain.
In silence shared, our hearts unite,
Through sorrow's song, we find the light.

For every life, a story told,
In echoes sweet, the memories hold.
Together we embrace the night,
In mourners' symphony, we find our might.

Lamentations Transformed

In shadows deep, our hearts do weep,
Yet hope arises, promises we keep.
Through trials painful, our spirits soar,
God's light breaks forth, forevermore.

Turn tears to joy, in grace we find,
In every struggle, love intertwined.
Wounds may linger, but strength is near,
In faith we stand, without fear.

Mountains tremble, the earth will shake,
Yet in His arms, we shall awake.
Broken dreams, yet visions clear,
In silent whispers, He draws us near.

From ashes rise, a new dawn glows,
In mercy's river, the spirit flows.
Lament transformed, in beauty's kiss,
Life renewed, a sacred bliss.

The Gospel of Renewal

Awake, O heart, to morning's grace,
In every breath, His love we trace.
Fields of promise, blooming bright,
The gospel sings, igniting light.

Chains are broken, burdens shed,
By faith we rise, where angels tread.
In every valley, His voice we hear,
Guiding us forth, dispelling fear.

From dust to life, we seek the way,
In each small moment, hope will stay.
Renewed in spirit, our mission clear,
To heal the world, to bring Him near.

With open hands, we share our gifts,
In every kindness, the spirit lifts.
The gospel flows, a river wide,
In love united, we shall abide.

Through trials faced, our hearts are bold,
In stories shared, His truth unfolds.
A tapestry of grace and light,
Forever woven, day and night.

Surrendering the Shadow

In stillness found, surrender lays,
The shadows fade, as light displays.
A heart laid bare, with fears released,
In holy moments, peace increased.

The burdens worn, they disappear,
In gentle whispers, truths draw near.
The night departs, the dawn awakes,
In surrendering, our spirit breaks.

Yet in the darkness, light remains,
In every struggle, love sustains.
With open arms, we let Him in,
To mend the heart, to cleanse from sin.

Let shadows fall, embrace the light,
A journey forged, in faith's insight.
Each step we take, a chance to grow,
In surrender sweet, His love we know.

Embracing grace, we find our way,
Through every trial, come what may.
Shadow surrendered, soul set free,
In love's embrace, our destiny.

Steps Toward the Sacred

Each step we take, a path to grace,
In every moment, we find our place.
With open hearts and willing hands,
Together bright, the spirit stands.

Through hidden trails, the journey calls,
With faith as guide, the heart enthralls.
In every challenge, lessons speak,
In silence deep, our spirits seek.

Gathering strength from trials past,
In every storm, we shall hold fast.
The sacred whispers, soft yet clear,
Guiding our steps, dispelling fear.

In gratitude, we lift our song,
For every wound, we'll learn to long.
Steps toward sacred, hand in hand,
Together we rise, united we stand.

With every breath, our spirits yearn,
In love's embrace, for truth we learn.
Steps taken boldly, a holy quest,
In Him, we find our hearts at rest.

Sanctity in the Silence

In the hush of dawn's soft light,
Whispers of the soul take flight,
Peace envelops the weary heart,
In quietude, we find our part.

Moments still, where dreams reside,
A sacred space, our hearts as guide,
In the silence, grace unfolds,
A tale of love, forever told.

Stars above in velvet night,
Kissing us with purest light,
Here we breathe, and hope ignites,
In the calm, our spirit fights.

Every prayer a gentle plea,
Echoes of eternity,
In the tranquil, we are whole,
United in a single soul.

Sanctity in every breath,
Life renewed in love, not death,
In stillness, we find our way,
Guided by the light of day.

The Promise of Tomorrow

With every dawn, a new embrace,
Hope awakens, time and space,
The promise written in the sky,
A whisper sweet, we learn to fly.

Hands united, hearts aglow,
Together, through the ebb and flow,
In faith we walk, come joy or sorrow,
Each step we take brings bright tomorrow.

Even shadows fall so deep,
Light will pierce; our souls to keep,
A future bright with love's refrain,
In every loss, there's more to gain.

Winds of change will bittersweet,
Yet faith remains, so strong, complete,
In every challenge, courage grows,
The promise of tomorrow glows.

Hear the call; let spirit rise,
Trust in light that never dies,
With every dream, in hope we soar,
The promise held forevermore.

Beneath the Weight of Heaven

In the quiet, burdens press,
Yet in love, we find our rest,
Beneath the weight of heaven's grace,
We wander forth, a noble race.

Through trials fierce, the spirit bends,
A tapestry of broken ends,
But woven strong, the heart shall mend,
In faith, the journey won't suspend.

Each tear that falls, like sacred dew,
Nourishes the soul anew,
In every struggle, light will gleam,
A thread of hope in every dream.

Though shadows loom and darkness calls,
A gentle hand, our spirit stalls,
With every breath, we rise again,
Beneath the weight, the love we gain.

In quiet moments, we attune,
To heavenly songs, soft as a tune,
In unity, we hold the key,
To lift our hearts and souls set free.

Wings of Serenity

Gentle breezes, whispers pure,
In every heart, we find the cure,
Wings unfold with grace divine,
In stillness, love and peace align.

In the garden where hope blooms,
Radiance dispels all the glooms,
Every petal, a prayer sent,
In love's embrace, our spirits bent.

Mountains high, valleys deep,
In our faith, we dare to leap,
With wings of serenity, we learn,
To rise above and brightly burn.

Though storms may rage and shadows cast,
The light of love will hold us fast,
In unity, the bond is strong,
With wings of faith, we sing our song.

So let us dance beneath the stars,
Healing wounds from distant wars,
With every heartbeat, joy is near,
Wings of serenity, let us steer.

Whispers of Grace

In quiet moments, angels sing,
Softly bringing joy to sting.
A gentle touch upon the heart,
From shadows of despair, we part.

The morning light breaks through the haze,
Illuminating hidden ways.
With every prayer, a hope restored,
A sacred bond, our spirits soared.

In trials faced, we learn to bend,
With faith unyielding, we transcend.
The whispers guide us to the light,
In darkest hours, they shine so bright.

Compassion flows like rivers wide,
In every tear, love will abide.
Embraced by grace, we find our place,
In every life, a holy space.

Together we rise, hand in hand,
United in truth, we take our stand.
With hearts of courage, we will trace,
The path of light - our whispers of grace.

The Dawn Beyond Sorrow

When night descends and shadows creep,
Awake my soul, from sorrow steeped.
In silence, hear the promise made,
A dawn of joy, no longer weighed.

The sun will rise with golden beams,
To heal the hearts and mend the seams.
In every tear, a lesson grows,
Through every trial, the spirit knows.

Hope is the fire that burns anew,
In every loss, a path laid true.
Through valleys deep, the light will flow,
To guide us where the rivers go.

Unfold the wings of weary dreams,
Embrace the warmth of love that beams.
The dawn will break, our fears will cease,
In faith, we find eternal peace.

With hands uplifted, hearts will sing,
A symphony of hope we bring.
Through every sorrow, we will see,
The dawn beyond, our destiny.

When Light Breaks the Veil

In shadows cast by doubt and fear,
A tender light draws ever near.
With faith unwound, let darkness flee,
When light breaks forth, we're truly free.

The veil of night begins to part,
Revealing truth within the heart.
In every soul, a spark ignites,
A beacon bold, through endless nights.

With whispered prayers, we rise as one,
In every battle fought and won.
Our hearts, a canvas painted bright,
When love ascends, we see the light.

Together in this sacred space,
We dance with joy, each step a grace.
For every wound, a healing balm,
When light breaks forth, the world feels calm.

United in this heavenly glow,
Our spirits soar, we come to know.
When light breaks through, we stand revealed,
In love's embrace, our souls are healed.

Healing Waters of the Soul

In tranquil tides, the spirit flows,
With healing waters, love bestows.
Through every wave, let burdens lift,
In gentle currents, find the gift.

A fountain springs from depths within,
To wash away the weight of sin.
With every drop, a whisper speaks,
Restoring hope for weary weeks.

Embrace the grace that fills your heart,
From sacred wells, we will not part.
In rivers shared, we find our peace,
Through healing waters, fears release.

With open arms, the light will shine,
Transforming tears to drops of wine.
In every splash, a love unbound,
In waters deep, true life is found.

Together we dive, hand in hand,
In flowing grace, we understand.
The healing waters cleanse the soul,
In holy tides, we are made whole.

Chronicles of Divine Kindness

In shadows deep, Your light does shine,
A path so clear, with love divine.
Each whispered prayer, a gentle song,
Through trials faced, we still belong.

With every tear, Your hand we feel,
The wounds of life, You gently heal.
In moments bleak, Your promise stays,
Guiding our hearts through endless days.

Your mercy flows like rivers wide,
A constant source, our trust, our guide.
In hearts of stone, You plant anew,
Compassion blooms, as hope breaks through.

Oh, let us dwell within Your grace,
In every time, in every place.
For kindness taught, we learn to share,
To lift the lost, to show we care.

With every breath, Your love we seek,
Through gentle words, through voices meek.
In unity, we find our way,
With grateful hearts, we all shall pray.

The Eternal Embrace of Grace

In quiet moments, You draw near,
An endless love, dispelling fear.
Through trials faced and burdens borne,
Your gentle hug, in sorrow, worn.

When storms arise, and doubts will creep,
Your endless arms, our souls do keep.
Through darkest nights, You light the way,
A steadfast hope, come what may.

In every step, Your grace does flow,
With every challenge, faith we sow.
In brokenness, You make us whole,
Restoring peace to every soul.

Your whispers soft, a tender balm,
In chaos loud, You bring us calm.
With open hearts, we seek to find,
The endless grace that soothes the mind.

Forever bound in love's embrace,
In every trial, we know Your face.
With hearts aligned, we rise above,
In every moment, we feel Your love.

The Sanctum of Healing

In the quiet hall, we gather,
Hearts lifted in solemn prayer.
Grace pours like water,
Quenching our deepest despair.

The light of hope glimmers bright,
Wrapping us in its warm embrace.
Here, souls mend in sacred sight,
Finding peace in this holy space.

Voices merge in harmonious song,
Each note a balm for the soul.
Together, we are ever strong,
In faith, we feel truly whole.

With every tear that we shed,
The burdens of life fade away.
In this haven, love is spread,
Guiding us to a new day.

So let us dwell in this grace,
United beneath heaven's dome.
In the sanctum we find our place,
In the heart of our eternal home.

Moments of Divine Intermission

In stillness, we pause and breathe,
An interlude blessed by the divine.
Every worry we gently cleave,
Trusting in love's sacred design.

A whisper echoes through the night,
Gentle reminders of His care.
In these moments, everything's right,
Our burdens lifted, light as air.

Clouds of doubt drift far away,
Raindrops of grace wash us clean.
In silence, we kneel and pray,
Finding solace in spaces unseen.

Time softens, the world stands still,
Our hearts open to healing light.
Each moment of peace, a holy thrill,
Guided by faith's steady sight.

With each intermission we see,
The threads of hope gently intertwine.
In this sacred pause, we can be,
Embraced by love, eternally divine.

Pilgrimage of the Brokenhearted

We walk the path of shadows cast,
With heavy hearts, we begin the quest.
Each step a reminder of the past,
In search of solace, we look for rest.

Tears like rivers flow unrestrained,
A language known to the aching heart.
In pain, we find the love unfeigned,
Strengthened by the wounds that impart.

Among the thorns, we find the grace,
In the darkest hour, a glimmer shines.
In every struggle, we trace His face,
As mercy, like sunlight, entwines.

The journey we take through mist and mire,
Transforms our loss into sacred gain.
With faith, we fan the flickering fire,
Turning our sorrow into refrain.

At the end of this pilgrimage made,
We'll find the love that never parts.
In every tear, the truth displayed,
We rise anew, mending our hearts.

The Sacred Whisper of Comfort

In the hush, a gentle voice calls,
Softly woven through our strife.
A tender touch in darkness falls,
Reminding us of the gift of life.

Through trials vast and mountains high,
This whisper wraps us in its grace.
No need to fear the storms that fly,
For we are always in His embrace.

Each echo brings a balm of peace,
A promise of love through every tear.
In quiet moments, fears release,
And hope breathes in every sphere.

We gather strength from sacred words,
Embracing all that love imparts.
In unity, our hearts like birds,
Soar together, healed in parts.

Here lies comfort, softly spoken,
In every heartache, joy is spun.
With faith, the silence is unbroken,
A testament that love has won.

Rivulets of Compassion

In the heart where kindness dwells,
Soft whispers flow, like gentle bells.
Each tear a stream of love expressed,
In sacred moments, souls find rest.

Through hands that heal and hearts that care,
Compassion's light is rich and rare.
For every burden shared in grace,
A touch of heaven's warm embrace.

In shadows deep, where silence sings,
The river flows, and hope takes wings.
We gather then, in unity,
To weave a world of harmony.

Each act of love, a sacred vow,
In the present, God is now.
With every gesture, joy will grow,
As rivulets of compassion flow.

Gathering the Fragments

Each shattered piece holds stories vast,
Of trials faced and shadows cast.
In brokenness, a chance to find,
The threads of love that tie mankind.

With hands outstretched, we gather near,
Embracing all that's held so dear.
In every crack, the light breaks through,
A tapestry of love, anew.

Through sorrow shared, we rise and mend,
In unity, we find our blend.
Together we create a whole,
Each fragment brings us to our goal.

In quiet moments, we reflect,
The beauty found in each defect.
For every piece, a lesson true,
A path to grace, for me and you.

Blessed Be the Broken

For in the cracks, where light does shine,
A sacred truth, a love divine.
Blessed are the hearts that bear the weight,
In all our trials, we find fate.

From burdens borne, we rise anew,
In each dark season, joy breaks through.
The broken shards reflect the light,
In every struggle, faith ignites.

With hands of grace, we mend the seams,
Creating hope from shattered dreams.
In every wound, a story told,
Of love that nurtures, brave and bold.

So let us gather, broken yet whole,
United in spirit, one shared soul.
For through our pain, we learn to see,
The blessed gift in fragility.

In the Silence of Reflection

In quietude, the spirit speaks,
A gentle whisper, calmness peaks.
Within the heart, a sacred space,
Where time stands still, and fears erase.

In the silence, wisdom grows,
Like fragrant blooms, a tranquil rose.
Each thought a prayer, each breath a song,
In stillness found, we all belong.

With eyes closed tight, we see the past,
In moments cherished, love holds fast.
For in the depths of silent grace,
We find the home, a warm embrace.

From shadows cast, new light will rise,
To guide our steps, to open skies.
In every silence, truth unfolds,
A journey rich, as love beholds.

Echoes of Mercy

In shadows deep, I seek your grace,
Your love a hand, my heart's embrace.
Forgive my faults, my wayward strays,
In every breath, your mercy stays.

With open arms, you gather near,
A whispered prayer, divinely clear.
Lost in the night, I find my way,
With echoes of mercy, brightening day.

In trials faced, I feel your call,
Your gentle touch, I rise and fall.
Through stormy seas, your beacon shines,
In every heart, your love aligns.

Together we walk, through grief and pain,
In every loss, your joy remains.
Lifted in spirit, we soar above,
In the embrace of endless love.

As dawn awakes, the shadows flee,
Your light prevails, it sets me free.
With grateful hearts, we start anew,
In echoes of mercy, forever true.

A Prayer for New Beginnings

Oh Lord, I stand at dawn's first light,
A spirit renewed, a heart alight.
With faith unshaken, I seek your face,
In every moment, I find your grace.

Guide my steps on paths unknown,
In every trial, I am not alone.
With courage bright, I face the day,
In your embrace, I find my way.

Bless this journey, let hope reside,
In whispers soft, you are my guide.
As blossoms bloom in springtime's breath,
I rise anew, defying death.

Each heartbeat sings of love divine,
In every challenge, your will, I align.
With prayers aflame, I lift my voice,
In faith I trust, I make my choice.

Oh Lord of grace, my heart's desire,
Ignite within me a sacred fire.
With open hands, I give my all,
In this new beginning, I heed your call.

From Ashes to Ascension

In ashes lie my dreams of old,
Yet from this dust, I rise so bold.
With every breath, a new refrain,
From trials faced, I break the chain.

Your guiding light, it leads my soul,
In darkened places, you make me whole.
With every tear, a seed is sown,
From pain and loss, my strength has grown.

Amongst the ruins, hope takes flight,
With wings of faith, I soar in light.
No fear can bind, no sorrow stay,
In grace I find, the brighter way.

From every setback, I emerge bright,
In shadows past, I find the light.
With open heart, I rise anew,
From ashes to ascension, my spirit true.

So here I stand, my head held high,
In reverent prayer, my soul will fly.
Together with you, I'll stand and sing,
From ashes to ascension, I am your being.

The Light That Follows Night

When darkness falls, and hope seems lost,
In silent prayers, I weigh the cost.
Yet through the veil, your promise gleams,
The light that follows all my dreams.

In every shadow, your love abides,
A gentle touch, where pain resides.
Through barren lands, your whispers flow,
With every dawn, my spirit glows.

As night gives way to morning's grace,
I find my strength, in your embrace.
Each moment shared, no fear shall reign,
In trials faced, I break the chain.

From shadows deep, your warmth will rise,
The light you bring, it never dies.
Through faith and trust, I'll carry on,
In love's embrace, the night is gone.

So let my heart reflect your light,
Through every struggle, through every fight.
In joyous song, my soul takes flight,
With you beside me, I'll find the light.

Radiance from the Ruins

From ashes rise, a light bestowed,
In shattered hearts, new hope is sowed.
Through darkest nights, His mercy streams,
In every soul, redemption gleams.

The past may haunt, yet grace draws near,
With every cry, He calms our fear.
In silence deep, His voice we find,
Renewed in spirit, hearts unconfined.

A tapestry of pain and love,
Woven beneath the stars above.
In brokenness, we learn to see,
The radiance of eternity.

Each step we take, a sacred dance,
Through trials faced, we find our chance.
Together in spirit, hand in hand,
We rise anew, to take a stand.

From ruins born, a faith refined,
In light and grace, our souls aligned.
With every breath, we choose to trust,
From ruins rise, in Him we must.

Love's Eternal Return

In every heart, a seed of grace,
A promise made, in love's embrace.
Through trials deep, we journey on,
In shadows cast, we find the dawn.

With open arms, He calls us home,
Through every storm, we're not alone.
In every tear, a story shared,
In truth and light, our souls prepared.

Beyond the night, the morning breaks,
In love's refrain, our spirit wakes.
Through grace bestowed, we find our way,
In every moment, love will stay.

The echoes of the past we hold,
In wisdom gained, our hearts are bold.
In faith's embrace, we rise anew,
Love's eternal dance we pursue.

In every life, a spark divine,
In sacred bond, our paths align.
Forevermore, in love we dwell,
In every heartbeat, truth we tell.

Upon the Rock of Faith

Upon the rock, our spirits stand,
In trials faced, we trust His hand.
Through life's rough waves, we find our way,
In faith we walk, by light of day.

In every storm, we seek His grace,
With steadfast hearts, we find our place.
From depths of fear, His voice we hear,
With courage strong, we conquer fear.

In prayer we rise, our burdens laid,
In silent whispers, peace conveyed.
With every step, the path grows clear,
In hope renewed, we draw Him near.

An anchor firm, in trials we face,
His love the fortress, our saving grace.
Through storms we pass, yet never stray,
Upon the rock, we choose to stay.

In faith united, we journey forth,
With hearts ablaze, we claim our worth.
Together strong, we fight the fight,
Upon the rock, we walk in light.

Shadows Lifting in Prayer

In the quiet night, our voices rise,
In humble hearts, we share our cries.
The shadows cast, they slowly fade,
In prayer's embrace, our fears are laid.

With open hands, we seek the light,
In every whisper, seeks the right.
Through trials faced, His love remains,
In every tear, our hope sustains.

The burdens lifted, grace descends,
In unity, our spirit bends.
Through darkest times, we stand as one,
In prayers we weave, new life begun.

In every heart, a gentle spark,
Through every dawn, dispelling dark.
In faith we stand, our spirits soar,
In shadows lifting, we grow more.

For every prayer, a bridge we form,
In every storm, He is the calm.
Together strong, our souls ignite,
In shadows lifting, we find light.

In the Arms of Faith

In shadows deep, we seek Thy light,
With gentle grace, our spirits rise.
In trials faced, we stand upright,
Thy love, O Lord, our heart's true prize.

With open arms, we find our peace,
In whispered prayers, our hopes ascend.
In every struggle, fears release,
Our faith, O Light, shall never bend.

Through darkest nights, Thy presence near,
A guiding star, our burdens bear.
In faith's embrace, we have no fear,
For in Thy love, we find our care.

So let us walk, hand in hand,
Through valleys low, to mountains high.
With faith our anchor, we will stand,
In Thy great love, we learn to fly.

In trials bold, Thy strength our shield,
In every moment, we are one.
In the arms of faith, hearts healed,
We rise renewed, like morning sun.

The Dawn of Healing

A new dawn breaks, the shadows flee,
With gentle rays, Thy light doth shine.
In fields of grace, we long to be,
Where hope and love intertwine.

As hearts now mend, we rise anew,
In sacred stillness, souls set free.
Thy tender hands, healing true,
Guide us to where we're meant to be.

In prayerful moments, comfort flows,
With every breath, we seek Thy way.
The dawn of healing softly glows,
Awakening peace in the light of day.

Through trials faced on paths unknown,
We find Thy mercy, pure and near.
In whispers sweet, our fears are flown,
The dawn of healing calms our fear.

With every heartache, tears once shed,
In love's embrace, we find our song.
A testament, Thy grace widespread,
In the dawn of healing, we belong.

Mending the Soul's Fabric

In threads of love, our souls we weave,
With every stitch, a prayer set free.
In brokenness, we shall believe,
Thy guiding hand, our certainty.

Through trials faced, each tear defines,
The beauty found in mending hearts.
In sacred love, our spirit shines,
As from the dark, new life imparts.

In gentle hands, the fabric whole,
Each moment cherished, each breath a gift.
From shattered dreams, we find our role,
With faith restored, our spirits lift.

With every bond, a sacred thread,
We weave our story, strong and bright.
In unity, no heart shall dread,
For love withstands the darkest night.

Through life's great loom, we find our place,
In mending hearts, our tale unfolds.
In faith we trust, in love, we brace,
For every soul, a truth retolds.

A Psalm for the Grieved

In sorrow's grip, we raise our voice,
A psalm of hope, through tears shall flow.
In darkest times, we still rejoice,
For in Thy love, we learn to grow.

Though grief may linger, peace shall dawn,
With every tear, a story shared.
In memories sweet, our spirits drawn,
In love's embrace, we've not despaired.

For every soul that leaves our sight,
In hearts they dwell, forever near.
In whispered prayers, we find the light,
To guide us through the weight of fear.

In every loss, a lesson learned,
A gentle strength within us blooms.
Through pain endured, our hearts have turned,
To find the light that love consumes.

A psalm for those who grieve today,
In trust, we lay our burdens down.
With faith, we'll find a brighter way,
In every heart, the love we've found.

The Altar of Acceptance

At the altar where we kneel,
Hearts laid bare, truth revealed.
In this sacred space we stand,
Holding faith within our hands.

Whispers echo through the night,
Guiding souls toward the light.
Every flaw, a gift divine,
In acceptance, we align.

Tears of joy, the burdens shed,
In forgiveness, love is spread.
Together we will rise and sing,
In acceptance, transformation brings.

Through the trials, we will find,
Unity of heart and mind.
Embracing all, we take our place,
In the warmth of heaven's grace.

With humble hearts, we now confess,
In surrender, we are blessed.
To the altar, we return,
Finding peace in love, we learn.

Rebirth in the Spirit's Embrace

In the quiet of the dawn,
New beginnings gently drawn.
Seasons change, a cycle spun,
In the spirit, we are one.

Every moment, fresh and bright,
Guided by the inner light.
From the ashes, hope takes flight,
Rebirth comes in grace's sight.

Life's sweet journey we explore,
Opening every sacred door.
In the embrace, we are restored,
In the spirit, love outpoured.

From struggles past we now arise,
With faith as vast as azure skies.
In the heart, a fire burns,
In the spirit, each soul yearns.

Boundless joy, the promise made,
In the love, no fear can shade.
Through every trial, we seek space,
In rebirth, we find our place.

Serenity's Gift

In the stillness, calm unfolds,
Whispers soft, high and bold.
With every breath, we come alive,
In serenity, we thrive.

Morning dew on petals fair,
Nature's peace beyond compare.
In the quiet, we can see,
All creation set us free.

Gentle streams and skies so blue,
Heaven's canvas, pure and true.
In the heart, a soothing balm,
Serenity, our souls' calm.

Through the chaos, we will roam,
Finding solace, making home.
In the stillness, spirits lift,
In life's journey, serenity's gift.

With gratitude, each moment passed,
In this peace, we find joy cast.
In harmony, we learn to live,
In serenity, forever give.

Grace Unveiled

In shadows cast by doubt and fear,
Grace emerges, ever near.
A gentle hand upon our heart,
In every moment, a new start.

Through the trials, we are shown,
In our weakness, grace is grown.
Every stumble leads us north,
In each lesson, we find worth.

Voices rise in song of praise,
Celebrating life's wondrous ways.
With open eyes, behold the sun,
In grace unveiled, we are one.

Mountains high and valleys low,
In this journey, love will flow.
Every heartbeat, a sacred rite,
In grace's arms, we find our light.

Through the tapestry we weave,
In each thread, we learn to believe.
Boundless mercy, pure as dove,
In grace unveiled, we find love.

In the Shadow of Redemption

In shadows deep, where grace does dwell,
A whisper soft, like sacred bell.
Hearts once lost, now found in light,
Guide us through the longest night.

Forgiveness blooms, a precious gift,
From heavy burdens, souls do lift.
Each step we take, His love our shield,
In faith and hope, our fate is sealed.

The broken chains, they fall away,
In mercy's arms, we humbly pray.
With every breath, we seek His face,
In trials strong, we find our grace.

Redeemed by grace, our spirits soar,
In Christ alone, we're evermore.
The path of light, forever leads,
To waters calm, where love proceeds.

The Resurrection of Hope

In silence deep, the stone was rolled,
A story new, of faith retold.
From grief and pain, a light will rise,
Transcending dark, to grace the skies.

Hope's gentle flame ignites the night,
Illuminating all that's right.
In hearts once torn, now healed anew,
A promise firm, in love so true.

Where doubt resides, let faith take flight,
For every wrong shall meet the right.
The empty tomb, a sign of grace,
Our souls renew in His embrace.

From ashes rise, a vibrant bloom,
In every heart, dispelling gloom.
With humble hearts, we lift our praise,
In resurrection's warm embrace.

The Garden of Broken Dreams

In gardens wild, where shadows creep,
Lie dreams once sown, now buried deep.
Yet from the soil of grief and woe,
New blossoms rise, in gentle glow.

Tears like rain, they water ground,
In suffering's grasp, new hope is found.
Through whispered prayers, the heart does mend,
In faith's embrace, we find a friend.

From bitter roots, sweet fruits will grow,
A love divine, we come to know.
With every storm, a chance to dream,
In brokenness, our spirits gleam.

This garden rich, of life and strife,
Embraces all, its breath of life.
In faithful hands, the seeds we sow,
In hope's great light, our spirits grow.

Blossoms in the Temple

In sacred halls, where spirits rise,
The scent of truth fills up the skies.
Each whispered prayer, a sacred breath,
In faith we stand, defying death.

With open hearts, we gather near,
In unity, we cast out fear.
The songs of angels fill the air,
In love's own light, we find our care.

The temple blooms with vibrant grace,
Each flower speaks of love's embrace.
Our seasons change, but faith remains,
Through trials faced, compassion gains.

In every stone, a story told,
Of hope and love, both brave and bold.
Together we rise, strong and free,
In blossoms bright, our unity.

A Symphony of Grace

In the stillness, prayers arise,
Hearts entwined beneath the skies.
Mercy flows like gentle streams,
Filling souls with softest dreams.

Wounds unbound by love's embrace,
Hope restored in sacred space.
Voices lift, a pure refrain,
Harmony amidst the pain.

Through the trials, faith will guide,
In His mercy, we abide.
Grace unfolds like morning light,
Chasing shadows, setting right.

Every tear, a seed of peace,
In His arms, our joys increase.
In the quiet, healing grows,
Spirit's touch, as softly flows.

Life's tempest cannot sever,
Boundless love, our greatest treasure.
With each moment, trust we stake,
In His promise, hearts awake.

A symphony of grace and song,
In His presence, where we belong.
After storms, a tranquil sea,
In His love, we are set free.

Light Beyond the Shadows

In the darkness, hope ignites,
Guiding hearts to higher sights.
Faith embers quietly glow,
Showing us the way to go.

Every struggle, every trial,
Brings the light to help us smile.
From the ashes, we shall rise,
Finding strength in sacred ties.

Grace transcends the darkest night,
With a whisper, brings the light.
Trust the journey we must take,
In His love, we will not break.

Each tear shed becomes a pearl,
Glimmers of a changed world.
Through the pain, His voice we hear,
Promising to draw us near.

With His armor, fears will flee,
In His grace, we're truly free.
Light illuminates the way,
Guiding us to brighter day.

Redemption's Whisper

Softly falls redemption's call,
In our hearts, we hear it all.
Love that mends the broken seams,
Weaving life back into dreams.

When the night seems cold and long,
Faith will lift us, make us strong.
In the silence, truth will bloom,
Filling hearts, dispelling gloom.

Grace envelops our despair,
Reminding us He is there.
With each heartbeat, love's refrain,
Guides us gently through the pain.

Every sorrow, every sigh,
Closer to the clouds we fly.
Hearts once heavy, now rearranged,
In His presence, we are changed.

Whispers sweet as dawn unfolds,
Stories of His grace retold.
In redemption, we find peace,
From our burdens, sweet release.

Heavens Unveiled

In the morning, heavens gleam,
Whispers echo, Spirit's dream.
Through the veil, we glimpse the grace,
In His light, we find our place.

Every tear a holy gift,
In our struggles, spirits lift.
In the beauty wrapped in pain,
Joy emerges with the rain.

Faith's small spark ignites the soul,
Leading us toward the whole.
In the silence, truths unfold,
Stories of the brave and bold.

Every moment, love will flow,
Teaching us what we must know.
Through the shadows, hope will guide,
In our hearts, forever abide.

As we seek, His light prevails,
Breaking through, the heavens wail.
In His mercy, peace is spread,
Blessed are those who seek and tread.

Beyond the Grave of Grief

In shadows deep, where sorrows lay,
A whisper calls, light breaks the gray.
From silent tombs, hope starts to rise,
Eternal love, beyond the skies.

Each tear we shed, a bridge is built,
To cleanse the heart, to heal the guilt.
In every loss, a lesson found,
In heaven's grace, our souls unbound.

The memories, like stars, will gleam,
In darkest night, they form a beam.
With every breath, we honor thee,
Transcending pain, forever free.

Through valleys dark, we walk with faith,
In every step, divine embrace.
For grief, though heavy, cannot last,
In love's pure light, the shadows pass.

So let us rise, with spirits bold,
Embrace the dawn, the tales retold.
Beyond the grave, love still remains,
A sacred bond, through joys and pains.

Psalms of Renewal

When morning breaks with gentle grace,
Creation sings, our hearts embrace.
In every leaf, a promise grows,
In whispered prayers, love overflows.

The winds of change, they softly blow,
Reviving hope, in hearts we sow.
With every dawn, a chance to start,
New life unfolds, igniting heart.

In trials faced, we find our strength,
Through storms of doubt, we go the length.
In sacred texts, the truth declared,
Our spirits lift, in love we're bared.

From ashes rise, like phoenix flight,
In darkest hours, we seek the light.
For every end, a fresh beginning,
In grace we find, our souls are winning.

God's tapestry, with colors bright,
In every shade, we'll find our sight.
With gratitude, we sing this song,
In unity, where we belong.

The Mosaic of Memory

Fragments of life, like scattered stones,
In gentle hands, we build our homes.
Each memory, a vibrant hue,
A tapestry of me and you.

In laughter's echo, in silence deep,
The stories shared, in hearts we keep.
Through trials faced, our spirits blend,
In every moment, love transcends.

Past's gentle touch, a guiding hand,
In every scar, the strength to stand.
Time weaves on, in sacred flow,
Memories bloom, like flowers grow.

With every glance, a tale unfolds,
In whispered winds, our heartbeats hold.
The mosaic shines, a work divine,
In faith and hope, our souls entwine.

Together we walk, through time's embrace,
In love's reflection, we find our place.
In every thread, the future gleams,
A guided path fulfilled in dreams.

The Holy Ascent

Upon the mount, where spirits soar,
The path of light, forevermore.
With faith as guide, we climb the height,
In sacred silence, we find our sight.

Each step we take, in peace we tread,
With hearts ablaze, where angels led.
In trials faced, we find our might,
A journey blessed, through day and night.

The echoes sing of grace profound,
In every trial, our hopes unbound.
With open arms, the heavens greet,
In sacred bond, our souls complete.

The holy ascent, a sacred quest,
Where love abides, and hearts find rest.
In unity, we rise and sing,
Embracing all the joy life brings.

With every breath, we feel the call,
To rise above, together we'll stand tall.
The holy journey, forever bright,
In love's embrace, we find our light.

Threads of Light

In the silence, faith does weave,
Threads of light that we perceive.
Every shadow, hope ignites,
Guiding souls to higher flights.

With each prayer, a silver thread,
Stitching hearts that once were red.
Woven stories through the night,
Unfolding truth in gentle light.

In the tapestry of grace,
Every point, a sacred place.
Together, we find our way,
Underneath the dawn of day.

Light not hidden, but revealed,
In the dark, our wounds are healed.
Lifted voices, softly sing,
Praises rise to everything.

Threads will tear, yet still, we'll mend,
In the love that knows no end.
Gathered close, we will not part,
Bound by light within the heart.

Restoration in the Sacred Breath

In the quiet of our sighs,
Restoration breathes and tries.
Every moment filled with grace,
Washes shadows from our space.

Sacred whispers fill the air,
Carrying our deepest prayer.
Each inhale, a chance to grow,
Exhaling pain, letting go.

Within our being, rhythms flow,
In the stillness, love will show.
Harmony in every breath,
Life renewed beyond the death.

Here we gather, souls aligned,
In this moment, hearts unwind.
Breath of heaven, pure and bright,
Guides us through the darkest night.

With each pulse, the spirit sings,
Life restored as silence clings.
In the sacred, we shall find,
Peace, the doorway to the mind.

The Peace Within the Travail

Through trials deep, we wander still,
Yet within our hearts, we will.
Finding strength in every tear,
Peace emerges, calm and clear.

Mountains high and valleys low,
In the struggle, love will grow.
In the darkness, light prevails,
Hope sustains through all the trails.

Voices trembling, yet they rise,
Singing softly, ancient cries.
In the battle, hearts unite,
Finding courage in the fight.

When the journey feels so long,
In the silence, join the song.
With each step, the burden fades,
Grace descending, hope cascades.

Peace does linger, always near,
In the travail, have no fear.
For the path may twist and bend,
Love unfolds beyond the end.

Hallowed Ground of the Heart

In sacred spaces, love does dwell,
Hallowed ground where spirits swell.
Every heartbeat sings a prayer,
Echoing our joys and care.

Where the whispers of the trees,
Sway in harmony with ease.
In each rustle, voices blend,
Nature's hymn, our souls transcend.

Across the garden, hope will bloom,
In the sun, dispelling gloom.
Every flower, a sacred trust,
Turning ashes back to dust.

On this ground, we find our place,
Joined as one in sweet embrace.
Holding fast to love's design,
In our hearts, the light will shine.

As we gather, hand in hand,
Together, we can understand.
In the hallowed, hearts align,
Finding solace in the divine.

Verses of Transformation

In shadows deep, a whisper calls,
The soul awakens, breaking walls.
With every trial, we rise anew,
In faith's embrace, we find what's true.

Old burdens shed, like leaves in fall,
A journey starts, we heed the call.
The heart's rebirth, a sacred dance,
In love's pure light, we take our chance.

The storms may rage, winds may howl,
Yet through the dark, we hear the soul.
With every step, the path aligns,
In trust we walk, as truth defines.

Each moment waits with grace to share,
From ashes rise, our spirits flare.
The past can teach, but does not bind,
In every breath, new hope we find.

So let us change, as seasons flow,
With open hearts, together grow.
In transformation, life unfolds,
The sacred story yet untold.

Clarity in the Chaos

In the storm's embrace, find the calm,
A quiet prayer, a healing balm.
In tangled thoughts, let silence reign,
In faith's soft light, dissolve the pain.

The world spins fast, yet here we stand,
In stillness found, we understand.
Through swirling doubts, the heart will lead,
In gentle whispers, plant the seed.

For every tear, a lesson dear,
Through trials faced, we must persevere.
With each dawn's light, our vision clears,
Embrace the truth, dismiss the fears.

The ebb and flow, a sacred dance,
In chaos wild, we take a chance.
The spirit guides where shadows creep,
In timeless love, a faith that's deep.

Through every storm, the sun will break,
In clarity's glow, we find our stake.
Together forged in trials faced,
In peace and light, our souls embraced.

Prayers for the Weary

O weary heart, in shadows dwell,
In life's great storm, all seems not well.
Yet in the silence, hear the plea,
A prayer for strength, for you and me.

With heavy burdens, we seek the light,
In darkest nights, come find your might.
The weary soul, a journey long,
Embrace the struggle, for you are strong.

Hands lifted high, we seek the grace,
In every tear, a sacred space.
For every challenge, surely come,
In faith's embrace, we are not done.

O gentle spirit, hear our cries,
In every breath, our hope still flies.
Through weary days, let love abound,
In every moment, let peace be found.

A prayer for strength, a wish for rest,
In life's embrace, we are truly blessed.
So let us walk, though weary still,
In love's sweet light, we find our will.

A Heart Wrapped in Light

In every shadow, find the spark,
A heart wrapped in light, ignites the dark.
With every breath, love's grace we weave,
In tender whispers, we believe.

A guiding star, through night so deep,
In heart's embrace, our dreams we keep.
Through trials faced, we understand,
In light we shine, together stand.

The warmth of hope, a gentle touch,
In love's embrace, we mean so much.
For every soul, a spark divine,
In unity found, our hearts entwine.

With every step, the journey's long,
In faith's pure strength, we can be strong.
Together in love, in light we thrive,
A heart wrapped in light, alive, alive!

In laughter shared and kindness shown,
We find our way, no longer alone.
So let love shine, with all our might,
In every heart, a glow so bright.

A Canopy of Mercy

Under the sky so wide and blue,
A gentle touch, a heart made new.
In every storm, the light breaks through,
With mercy's grace, our faith renews.

Wings of love, they softly soar,
Embracing those who seek once more.
In whispered prayers, our spirits dance,
Beneath the canopy of His glance.

From shadows deep, our souls align,
Bound by the thread of love divine.
Each step we take, in trust we find,
A path illuminated, redefining.

In quiet moments, hear the call,
A sacred journey, we rise or fall.
With mercy's hand, our burdens lift,
In every challenge, a holy gift.

Together we stand, hearts intertwined,
In unity, our spirits combined.
Within this grace, our hopes abound,
Forever in mercy, love is found.

From Ashes to Absolution

From ashes deep, a voice will rise,
An echo of faith, beyond the skies.
In every tear, a lesson learned,
From shadows cold, the heart has burned.

With fire's light, old burdens freed,
We journey forth, on love we feed.
In trials faced, we find our way,
From despair's grip, to a brighter day.

In humble whispers, grace descends,
A gentle nudge, the soul mends.
Through every scar, the light shines through,
Absolution granted, hearts anew.

From brokenness, we rise and stand,
With open hearts, we join His hand.
Each step we take, a sacred vow,
From ashes born, we praise Him now.

Renewed in spirit, we move ahead,
Trusting the path where angels tread.
From ashes deep, to love's embrace,
In every moment, we find His grace.

Seeds of Hope in Despair

In barren fields where shadows grow,
The seeds of hope begin to show.
With faith as light, we plant with care,
In every heart, a whispered prayer.

Through darkest nights, we seek the sun,
With hearts united, we are one.
For even in despair, we stand,
Holding together, hand in hand.

In trials faced, our spirits ignite,
A flame of love, guiding the night.
For every tear, a flower blooms,
In grace, we find a sweet perfume.

With every step, new dreams arise,
In unity, we touch the skies.
From seeds of hope, our futures grow,
In every heart, His love will flow.

In sacred silence, we hear His song,
A melody sweet, where we belong.
Amidst the storms, our faith we bare,
Sprouting love's seeds from deepest despair.

The Halo of Understanding

In quiet moments, wisdom speaks,
A halo bright, the heart it seeks.
With open minds, we learn to see,
The ties that bind humanity.

Through every trial, we come to know,
In shared struggles, our spirits grow.
Empathy blooms, a sacred bond,
In understanding, we rise beyond.

For in each soul, a story lies,
With gentle eyes, we hear the cries.
Compassion's light, it guides our way,
In every heart, love's soft bouquet.

Together we weave a tapestry,
Of dreams and hopes, a unity.
Under the halo, we find our place,
In each embrace, a warm embrace.

With hearts open wide, we gather near,
In the halo's glow, we cast out fear.
For understanding leads us home,
In love's embrace, we're never alone.

Grace in Brokenness

In shadows deep, we find a light,
A whisper soft, in darkest night.
With every tear, the heart does mend,
In brokenness, our souls transcend.

The weight we bear, a heavy yoke,
Yet from the ashes, hope awoke.
In humble prayer, we seek the grace,
To find the strength in our embrace.

From shattered dreams, new paths arise,
Though pain may linger, love defies.
In every scar, a story told,
Of faith and courage, brave and bold.

With every fall, we learn to rise,
In unity, our spirits fly.
As light breaks through, a dawn anew,
In grace, our hearts, forever true.

So let us walk, hand in hand,
In brokenness, together stand.
With open hearts, we'll sow the seeds,
Of healing love, for all our needs.

The Journey to Solace

Through valleys low, we wander far,
In search of peace, our guiding star.
With every step, the path is clear,
In whispered prayers, we draw them near.

The mountains high, they call our name,
In trials faced, we rise the same.
For solace waits, in hearts aligned,
In quiet strength, our souls entwined.

Through storms that rage, our spirits sing,
A melody of hope we bring.
With open hands, we seek the way,
In darkest nights, we find the day.

With every breath, the journey unfolds,
In every heart, a tale retold.
Together bound, in love we trust,
In sacred paths, we find what's just.

So let us walk, this journey wide,
With faith as guide, and hearts our pride.
In solace found, we learn to cope,
In every corner, shines our hope.

When Hearts Find Peace

In moments still, when silence reigns,
The heart discovers, calm remains.
With gentle breath, we find the way,
To let our worries fade away.

In nature's grace, we feel the flow,
As rivers run, our spirits grow.
In kindness shared, we find the ease,
As tender hearts embrace the peace.

Through trials faced, we learn to see,
The beauty in our unity.
When love surrounds, we grow as one,
In every heart, a battle won.

With open arms, we gather near,
In every laugh, we shed a tear.
For in the joy, we find release,
As all our troubles find their cease.

So let us share this sacred space,
Where every soul can find its place.
In every heart, a light does gleam,
When hearts find peace, we live the dream.

Beneath the Weeping Willow

Beneath the willow, shadows play,
In whispered winds, our thoughts convey.
With every branch, a story flows,
Of gentle hearts and all it knows.

The earth, it holds our silent tears,
In tender moments, calms our fears.
With roots that stretch, we find our ground,
In nature's arms, love's voice is found.

As leaves cascade like softest sighs,
In every flutter, hope complies.
The branches cradle, wisdom true,
In every heart, begins anew.

With open skies, we seek the vast,
In every lesson learned from past.
Beneath the willow, life unfolds,
In sacred peace, our truth beholds.

So let us gather, side by side,
In love's embrace, we shall abide.
With every dream, we write our song,
Beneath the willow, we belong.

The Promise of Tomorrow

In the dawn's gentle breath, we rise,
Hope whispers softly, amid the skies.
Every tear sheds light on a path,
Guided by grace, we embrace the aftermath.

Tomorrow's sun shall paint the land,
With colors of love, divine and grand.
Faith is the anchor in life's stormy sea,
Casting our doubts, we shall truly be free.

Each promise spoken, a sacred vow,
In stillness we listen, we know not how.
Moments of struggle, through shadows we tread,
The light of the future, our spirits are fed.

So walk with me on this sacred road,
In unity's strength, we shall share the load.
For every sunset, a rising awaits,
In the cycle of life, love perpetuates.

Let hearts be open to tomorrow's call,
For in each ending, a new dawn shall fall.
Together we journey, with souls intertwined,
The promise of tomorrow, forever enshrined.

Sacred Resilience

In the heart of the storm, we find our strength,
A spirit unbroken, we rise at length.
Through trials and sorrows, we learn to stand,
Guided by faith, we reach for His hand.

Each tear that we shed, a lesson we learn,
In sacred resilience, our spirits will burn.
Facing the tempest, we hold to our light,
In the depths of the night, we seek out the bright.

With every heartbeat, a testament true,
The power of love will carry us through.
Though shadows may linger, our hope will not cease,
In the arms of the Divine, we find our peace.

Together we gather, our hearts intertwined,
In the fabric of grace, our souls are aligned.
Through valleys of sorrow, we journey as one,
In sacred resilience, we flourish, we run.

For life is a blessing, a gift from above,
In every storm's fury, we witness His love.
With courage as armor, the future we face,
In sacred resilience, we find our place.

Lifting the Veil of Sorrow

Beneath the weight of grief, we sigh,
Yet through the darkness, we learn to fly.
In pain's embrace, the soul finds a song,
Through trials endured, we learn to be strong.

With every heartache, a lesson bestowed,
Each moment of silence, a sacred road.
Lifting the veil, we glimpse the divine,
In ashes of sorrow, new hopes intertwine.

The tears that we shed are rivers of grace,
Flowing gently, carving out space.
For love is the beacon that guides us through,
In lifting the veil, our spirits renew.

Amidst the shadows, a light still remains,
A whisper of comfort that eases our pains.
In unity's strength, we gather and heal,
Lifting the veil, our sorrows conceal.

Through heartache and loss, we will not despair,
For in every shadow, His presence is there.
With courage and faith, we shall overcome,
Lifting the veil, our hearts beat as one.

The Quietude of Regret

In the stillness of night, regret finds its voice,
Haunting the heart, it leaves us no choice.
Yet in the silence, a lesson unfolds,
For every misstep, a truth to behold.

With whispers of longing, we search for the past,
Understanding that moments are fleeting, not vast.
In the quietude of regret, we learn to forgive,
Embracing the shadows, we choose how to live.

Each choice that we made, a path carved in time,
The echoes of yesterdays blend into the rhyme.
In lessons of sorrow, our hearts are refined,
In the quietude of regret, solace we find.

Let not the weight of regret tear us apart,
For in every ending, a chance for new starts.
With grace in our hearts, we'll cherish what's near,
In the quietude of regret, we find peace, not fear.

So let us walk gently, with wisdom anew,
Embracing our journey, both the old and the new.
In the stillness, we gather the fragments of love,
The quietude of regret, a blessing from above.

Peace in the Midnight Hour

In the silence, whispers softly flow,
Hearts entwined in the moon's gentle glow.
Angels gather, their song weaves light,
Bringing calm to the depths of night.

In the stillness, the spirit will rise,
Casting out fears, where hope never dies.
A lullaby in the shadows we find,
Comforting all, the lost and the blind.

Through the darkness, a promise unfolds,
Love eternal, more precious than gold.
Rest in the grace that the night does impart,
A refuge, a balm for the weary heart.

Let each moment be quiet and clear,
In the midnight hour, God draws near.
Whispers of faith, like stars in the sky,
Guide us through night, never to die.

The Psalter of Hope

In the dawn of a new day, we rise,
Singing praises with hearts full of sighs.
Each verse a promise, a light that will beam,
Flowing like waters from a well of dreams.

With every struggle, our spirits entwine,
Finding strength in the love that's divine.
The rhythm of life, a sacred refrain,
Carrying burdens and washing the pain.

Let hope be the lantern that lights up our way,
Through valleys of shadows, come what may.
With joy unconfined in the trials we meet,
Faith will uplift us, no foe can defeat.

In the echoes of prayer, we stand as one,
Bound together, till victory's won.
With arms wide open, embrace the unknown,
For in every heartbeat, His grace is shown.

Beneath the Weight of Sorrow

When the clouds of despair begin to descend,
And the heart feels heavy, seeking to mend.
In the depths of our pain, we call to the Lord,
Finding solace and peace in His Word.

Though the night may feel endless, we'll stand tall,
On the strength of His love, we shall never fall.
With each tear that falls, He collects every sigh,
Turning burdens to blessings as time passes by.

In the shadow of grief, hope's flicker ignites,
Guiding us softly through long, sleepless nights.
For beneath every sorrow, a purpose awaits,
A story of healing that love celebrates.

Through trials and storms, we learn to embrace,
The lessons of life, His unending grace.
Through the weight of our sorrow, we rise from the dust,
Trusting in Him, the path we will trust.

Revealing the Hidden Blessings

In the stillness of heart, we seek to explore,
The treasures of life that lie at our door.
With eyes opened wide, let us look and see,
The beauty in all, in the vast tapestry.

In moments of kindness, grace softly flows,
In laughter and love, our spirit grows.
Every challenge we face illuminates,
The hidden blessings that life orchestrates.

With gratitude deep as the ocean is wide,
We find strength in faith, our unyielding guide.
Through the lens of His love, our worries subside,
Revealing the gifts that forever abide.

Let our hearts rejoice in the paths that we tread,
For in every sorrow, a blessing is bred.
In the light of His mercy, may we take our stance,
Cherishing each breath, in this sacred dance.

Threads of the Divine

In the fabric of the night, we find,
Stitches of light, in shadows entwined.
Each whisper, a thread, from heavens above,
Woven with care, in a tapestry of love.

In silence, the Spirit gently calls,
Echoing softly through the hallowed halls.
Guiding the heart with luminous grace,
Illuminating the sacred space.

A tapestry rich, with colors so bright,
Every soul's journey, a radiant plight.
With hands lifted high, we seek the true,
Threads of existence, connecting me and you.

In the dance of the stars, a story unfolds,
Of ancient wisdom and promises told.
Each moment a stitch in our divine fate,
A journey of faith, intricately straight.

Together we weave in this sacred design,
Finding our purpose, in love we align.
With threads of the divine, in harmony found,
We rise in the light, on holy ground.

Sanctuaries of Healing

In the stillness of night, the heart finds peace,
A sanctuary formed, where sorrows cease.
With open arms, the spirit aligns,
In the warmth of love, true healing shines.

In whispers of hope, the broken are whole,
A gathering place, where we mend the soul.
With every tear shed, new strength is born,
In the light of compassion, we embrace the dawn.

The hands of the faithful extend their grace,
Welcoming all to this sacred space.
With hearts intertwined, we share our plight,
Finding solace together, in the still of the night.

In the garden of faith, we plant our dreams,
Nurtured with love, in divine streams.
Each prayer a seed, in the soft earth sown,
In these sanctuaries, we're never alone.

As the sun rises high, casting shadows away,
We walk in the light, step by step, day by day.
In the warmth of our bonds, strength we reveal,
In these sanctuaries of healing, our spirits heal.

Gardens of Grace

Amidst the flowers, in colors so bright,
Gardens of grace bloom in morning light.
With each gentle breeze, whispers of love,
Echoing blessings from heavens above.

Soft petals of faith, unfolding their charm,
Embracing the weary, offering balm.
In the dance of the leaves, a sacred song,
In gardens of grace, we all belong.

Through trials of life, we cultivate trust,
Turning to soil, from ashes and dust.
Each moment of kindness, a seed we sow,
In the richness of spirit, our love will grow.

In the twilight hour, reflection takes flight,
Under the stars, we find our insight.
Gardens of grace, in silence they bloom,
Illuminating pathways, dispelling the gloom.

Together we wander, in nature's embrace,
Finding our purpose in this holy space.
In the fragrance of peace, our hearts intertwined,
In these gardens of grace, true love we find.

Rebirth in Faith

In the darkness, a spark ignites,
A flame of hope, as the spirit writes.
With each heartbeat, a new chance to be,
Rebirth in faith, setting the soul free.

From ashes we rise, like the dawn's first light,
Breaking the chains that bound us in night.
In surrender, we find a pathway revealed,
To the promises kept, our hearts gently healed.

Through valleys of doubt, we walk in trust,
In the arms of the light, our spirits adjust.
With courage, we stand, facing storms that rage,
Rebirth in faith, turning a new page.

As the world awakens, we breathe in grace,
Together we journey, each step we embrace.
In the rhythms of life, our spirits align,
In this sacred rebirth, the Divine we find.

With open hearts, we let go of the past,
In the beauty of now, we're anchored at last.
In the cycle of life, our souls take flight,
In rebirth of faith, we shine ever bright.

Pilgrimage of the Soul

Through valleys deep the spirit roams,
In search of peace and sacred homes.
With faith as light, the path is clear,
Each step a prayer, the heart sincere.

The mountains high, the rivers wide,
In silence speaks, the soul's guide.
With every breath, a whisper found,
In nature's arms, the truth unbound.

The stars above, a celestial scheme,
Awake the heart to holy dreams.
In twilight's glow, the spirit sways,
Entranced by love in endless praise.

Each soul a flame, a spark divine,
In unity we seek to shine.
Embracing light, we walk as one,
Together rise, till night is done.

Let every trial be sacred ground,
In every loss, a joy profound.
For on this road, we find the whole,
The journey is the pilgrimage of the soul.

In the Wake of God's Grace

In shadows cast, His light will break,
The weary find the strength to wake.
With every dawn, His mercy flows,
In every heart, His kindness grows.

The gentle hands, they lift us high,
Through every storm, He draws us nigh.
His whispers calm the raging sea,
A promise made, He walks with me.

Each tear we shed, a holy sign,
In love's embrace, our souls entwine.
Celestial grace, a tender guide,
In the wake of faith, we'll abide.

Through trials faced, we rise anew,
His endless love, forever true.
In gratitude, our spirits soar,
In the wake of grace, forevermore.

Revelations of a Healed Heart

In quiet moments, truth revealed,
The wounds of time, at last, are healed.
With open arms, we welcome peace,
In love's embrace, our sorrows cease.

The past releases its heavy chains,
In gentle whispers, hope remains.
Each scar a story, a journey told,
Of battles fought and hearts made bold.

From darkest nights, a dawn shall rise,
With healing light in tender skies.
In unity, we stand renewed,
Revelations born of gratitude.

With every breath, we sing His praise,
In gratitude, our spirits blaze.
In the sacred stillness, we find our start,
The joy that comes from a healed heart.

The Chalice of Comfort

In life's embrace, the chalice full,
With kindness deep, our hearts we pull.
In trials faced, we share the load,
In friendship's light, our spirits flowed.

The wine of joy, the bread of grace,
In every face, a sacred place.
With tender hands, we break the bread,
In loving hearts, our sorrows shed.

For even in the darkest night,
The chalice shines with hope's pure light.
In fellowship, we find our song,
In harmony, we all belong.

So raise the cup, and toast the day,
In gratitude, we learn to pray.
For life's a gift, a sacred part,
In every sip, the comfort of heart.

Celestial Echoes of Mercy

In the stillness of night, we pray,
Voices whisper of love, they say.
Clouds part to reveal a gentle light,
Guiding us through the depths of night.

Waves of grace wash over our souls,
Filling the void, making us whole.
Each heartbeat pulses a sacred song,
In the embrace where all belong.

From the heavens, mercy flows wide,
In sorrows sweet, we choose to bide.
With every trial, our spirits rise,
Finding hope in the tears we cry.

Angels dance in a celestial choir,
Igniting in us a divine fire.
Their presence kindles the faith we share,
In a world where love fills the air.

Let our lives be a testament clear,
As we walk, unafraid of fear.
For in each echo of mercy bestowed,
We find the path our hearts have strode.

The Promise of Daisies

In fields where daisies sway and gleam,
Lies the promise of a hopeful dream.
Each petal whispers a tale of grace,
Of love and peace in an endless space.

Beneath the sun, our spirits dance,
Embracing joy in every glance.
Nature sings of the life we lead,
In every flower, a sacred seed.

The earth cradles us in its embrace,
In this garden, we find our place.
Meditations on the beauty of now,
A spiritual vow to the sacred how.

As seasons shift, we learn to trust,
In the soil, we rise from dust.
Daisies nod with a gentle sway,
Reminding us of the brighter day.

With every bloom, a chance to grow,
To bask in love, to let it show.
In the symphony of life's ballet,
We discover hope in each new day.

Journey from Grief to Glory

Through shadows deep, our hearts did weep,
In silence profound, our souls did seek.
Yet within the pain, a light we'd find,
A whisper of love, gentle and kind.

Each tear we shed, a seed of grace,
We rise from ashes in time and space.
The road may twist, but here we stand,
With courage born from love's own hand.

The mountains loom, but we press on,
Guided by faith from dusk till dawn.
In every struggle, a story unfolds,
Of redemption and victory, a heart that holds.

With every breath, we take a stand,
Transcending grief, hand in hand.
For glory awaits in the rising sun,
A symphony played, our hearts as one.

Embracing the past, we step into light,
A journey of hope, taking flight.
Forever transformed, our spirits soar,
From grief to glory, forevermore.

Harmonics of the Heart's Ascent

In the stillness, our spirits hum,
A melody of love, a sacred drum.
Each note we sing lifts the soul high,
In harmony, we learn to fly.

With every heartbeat, the music swells,
Tales of grace that the heart compels.
In moments of joy and times of strife,
The chord of faith resonates with life.

As we climb towards the skies above,
The path is paved with endless love.
In the symphony of treasures untold,
We embrace the truth that never grows old.

Let compassion lead, let kindness reign,
In the concert of life, we break every chain.
With open hearts, we celebrate sound,
In the music of love, we are forever bound.

As we gather, souls intertwine,
In the rhythm of grace, our spirits align.
For in the ascent, we find our place,
In the harmonics of His endless grace.

Foundations of Forgiveness

In shadows cast by human plight,
We seek to mend with gentle heart.
Forgiveness rests like morning light,
Healing begins where love imparts.

Each prayer a bridge, we dare to cross,
To find the peace that lies within.
In grace, we count both gain and loss,
Together, free from guilt and sin.

With open arms, let burdens cease,
Embracing every faithful soul.
In unity, may we find peace,
Forgiveness makes the broken whole.

Through trials faced, the heart will learn,
That mercy flows like rivers wide.
In lovingkindness, hearts will yearn,
To share the grace, with arms spread wide.

In whispered hope, we lift our hands,
To seek the light that leads us forth.
Forgiveness, like a golden strand,
Binds all together, rich in worth.

Moments of Celestial Clarity

In twilight's glow, the heavens speak,
Where stars align in perfect grace.
Each breath a prayer, each thought unique,
We glimpse the truth, a holy space.

With open eyes, we seek the dawn,
As whispers guide the searching mind.
In moments brief, we feel reborn,
Where souls connect, divinely twined.

Clouds part to show the radiant glow,
Of love that binds, of faith we share.
In every heart, a seed will grow,
A gift of kindness, pure and rare.

The universe, a tapestry,
Weaving threads of joy and strife.
In clarity, we come to see,
Life whispers truth beyond this life.

And when the night falls firm and still,
We dance among the stars in prayer.
In sacred silence, hearts will fill,
With moments pure, beyond compare.

The Call of the Spirit

In quietude, I hear the call,
A sacred echo through the night.
The Spirit whispers, kind and small,
Inviting souls to rise in light.

With every breath, a promise made,
To seek the path of sacred trust.
In faith, our doubts begin to fade,
The heart awakens, pure and just.

Through trials faced, we climb the heights,
Each stumble teaches strength anew.
In unity, we find our rights,
Together, ever strong and true.

The Spirit's voice, a gentle guide,
Through valleys deep where shadows lie.
In service, joy and love abide,
With open hearts, we reach the sky.

And when the dawn will greet our eyes,
We'll know the grace from whom we came.
Each soul, a star that softly flies,
The Spirit's call, our endless flame.

The Reverent Rebirth

In darkened earth, the seed must dwell,
Awaiting warmth of grace divine.
From humble roots, we rise and swell,
In reverence, our hearts align.

The cycle spins, where life renews,
Each ending births a brand new start.
In stillness, search for sacred clues,
As faith ignites the weary heart.

From ashes, hope will always rise,
In storms of change, we find our way.
With open hearts and lifted eyes,
We greet the dawn, embrace the day.

In every trial, wisdom's gain,
The spirit learns to rise up high.
Through love's embrace, we break the chain,
In reverent rebirth, we will fly.

Each moment passed is not in vain,
For in our growth, the Light we find.
In every heart that breaks in pain,
A reverent rebirth, gently timed.

The Temple of Renewal

In quiet whispers, prayers ascend,
Lost souls seek, their hearts to mend.
Each stone a tale of past despair,
Yet grace abounds, we find it there.

Through open doors, the light pours in,
A breath of hope, where love begins.
In sacred space, our spirits rise,
As faith ignites, our fears demise.

The altar stands, a humble plea,
We lay our burdens, set them free.
In unity, our voices blend,
Together strong, as hearts we mend.

With every step, we seek the truth,
In youthful hearts, or aged in sooth.
The temple beckons, calling loud,
Awakening joy, amidst the crowd.

As dusk then dawn, we rise anew,
In every prayer, God's love shines through.
The temple of renewal stands,
A gift of grace, from His own hands.

Wings of a New Dawn

Awake, arise, the morning breaks,
On golden wings, our spirit wakes.
With every breath, we seek the light,
In shadows past, we find our sight.

The sun ascends, our fears take flight,
In fields of hope, we claim our right.
The world reborn, with every hue,
A canvas vast, our hearts made new.

Nature sings, a joyous choir,
Each note a spark, ignites the fire.
In every heart, a song resounds,
For wings of grace, in love, we're found.

Together we soar, hand in hand,
Over mountains high, through golden sand.
A journey shared, in faith we bask,
With open hearts, in prayer we ask.

As dawn unfolds, our lives entwined,
In sacred peace, true love defined.
With wings of grace, we're blessed above,
In every breath, we find His love.

The Altar of Acceptance

Upon this stone, we lay our shame,
In humble hearts, we call Your name.
We gather near, in quiet grace,
The altar stands, our sacred space.

With open hands, we greet the pain,
For in our struggles, we shall gain.
Forgiveness flows, like rivers wide,
In unity, we turn the tide.

Acceptance dwells, in every heart,
Through trials faced, we find our part.
In whispered prayers, we find our trust,
For love withstands, in faith we must.

Each tear that falls, a story told,
In warmth of love, we break the cold.
Together strong, we lift our song,
In every moment, we belong.

The altar glows, with hope renewed,
In every heart, His love imbued.
Through tears of joy, we find our grace,
At the altar of acceptance, a warm embrace.

The Sacred Thread of Joy

In laughter shared, the spirit twirls,
A sacred thread, through all our worlds.
With joyous hearts, we weave and dance,
In faith's embrace, we find our chance.

Each colorful strand, a blessing bright,
In unity, we shine with light.
Through trials faced, the fabric grows,
In love's warm glow, the beauty shows.

The tapestry binds, each soul a thread,
Through joy and pain, our hearts are led.
In gentle hands, we stitch our dreams,
With every hope, a love redeems.

So gather near, let laughter ring,
In every heart, let joy take wing.
With every stitch, in love we find,
The sacred thread, forever twined.

In moments small, the joy reveals,
In shared embraces, our spirit heals.
Together woven, we rise and sing,
In the sacred thread, our souls take wing.

Milton Keynes UK
Ingram Content Group UK Ltd.
UKHW031321271124
451618UK00007B/158